Comku Thoŋ de Jiëëŋ

John Awai Piok

A E I O U

A Note from the Publisher

The publisher wishes to acknowledge and thank Dr Douglas H. Johnson for his invaluable help and support for Africa World Books and its mission of preserving and promoting African cultural and literary traditions and history. Dr Johnson and fellow historians have been instrumental in ensuring that African people remain connected to their past and their identity. Africa World Books is proud to carry on this mission.

© John Awai Piok, 2021

ISBN: 978-0-6450944-4-2

All rights reserved.

No part of this publication may be reproduced, stored in a retrieval system, or transmitted, in any form, or by any means, electronic, mechanical, photocopying, recording or otherwise, without the prior permission of the publishers.

This book is sold subject to the conditions that it shall not, by way of trade or otherwise, be lent, re-sold, hired out or otherwise circulated without the publisher's prior consent in any form of binding or cover other than in which it is published and without a similar condition including the condition being imposed on the subsequent purchaser.

Cover design, typesetting and layout : Africa World Books

TABLE OF CONTENTS

Introduction	5
Acknowledgements	7
Chapter 1 Akeer Ke Thuɔŋjäŋ	9
Akeer ke Thuɔŋjäŋ	10
Akeerdït ku Akeerthi	23
Akeer Dheu	37
Akeer Yäu	51
Akeer Dhëŋ	65
Akeer Lɔc	75
Akeer Dheu ku Akeer Yäu	111
Chapter 2 Tök Ku Käjuëc	135
Tök ku Käjuëc	136
Chapter 3 Ruääi	165
Ruääi	166

Chapter 4 Kä Tɔ̈ Në Guɔ̈pic   173

Chapter 5 Wël Ku Jam   181

Wël ku Jam   182
Thiëc   227

Chapter 6 Kuɛ̈n   241

Kuɛ̈n   242
Mät   258
Mïïtbei   259
Tëk   260
Yup   261

INTRODUCTION

This book is written in Dinka language for the Dinka people and for all who might be wanting to learn more. The Dinka people are the largest group of all 63 tribes of South Sudan. The Dinka language, on other hands, is the third most spoken language in South Sudan after Arabic and English.

The Dinka language is deeply rooted in the tradition of the African people in that it was passed on orally from generations to generations. It is, therefore, fair to say that the Dinka Language is now the goldfield where our ancestors have deposited their wisdom, norms, and traditions. It is the duty of our most educated generation to invest time, energy and resources to develop the Dinka language. It is also our responsibility to ensure the Dinka language is made more accessible, more understandable, and more attractive and interesting to all.

This book is written in Brisbane Australia and named Comku Thoŋ de Jiëëŋ. The phrase "Comku Thoŋ de Jiëëŋ" is loosely translated in English as "Planting the Dinka Language." By using the word "planting," we are depicting the Dinka language as a seed in storage awaiting to be planted in a fertile soil. The soil is our community which we must encourage to read and write Dinka fluently. We must also take it as our ultimate responsibility to teach our children to read, write, and speak Dinka as if they were born in South Sudan.

ACKNOWLEDGEMENTS

I would like to give special thanks to James Kur Bol Nguet for his steadfast support and creativity which has been coming from the beginning to the end of this book. Surely, I would not have done it without his unflinching support and encouragement.

I also thank my brother Peter Lual Reech Deng and his team at the African World Books. I commend their encouragement and ability to shape simple thoughts and turn them into magnificent artistic work. May Almighty God shower His abundance blessings into their efforts and creativity.

Finally, I am dedicating this book to JWL Youth Ministry which has been the source of my strength and inspiration since I joined it as a Sunday School many years ago.

CHAPTER 1

Akeer Ke Thuɔŋjäŋ

Thoŋ de Jiëëŋ anɔŋic Akeer ke thiërou ku dhorou.

A   E

I  O  U

W  Y

P B M

N  NH

Ŋ NY R

D  DH

K

G

Y   c   J

Akeerdït ku Akeerthi

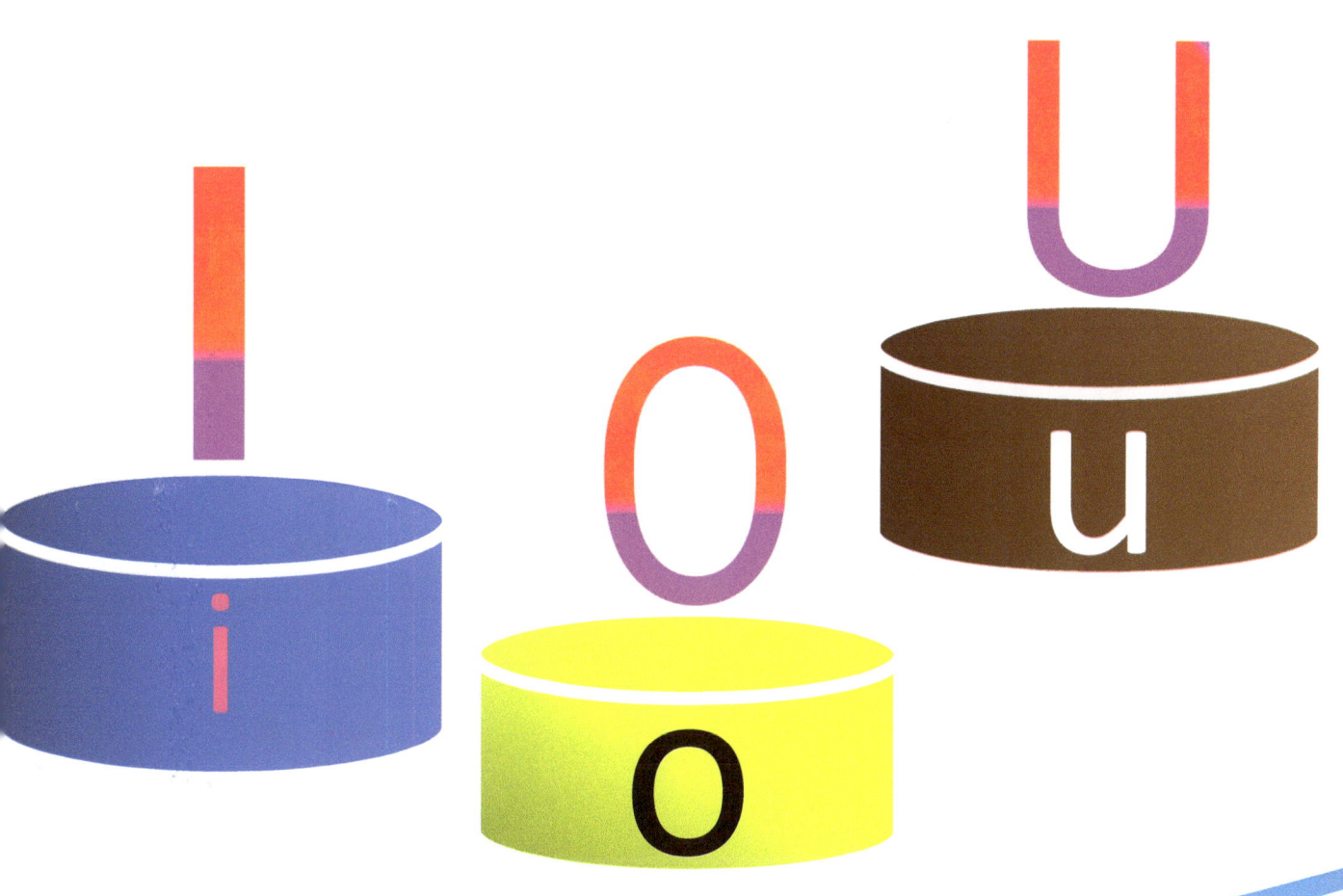

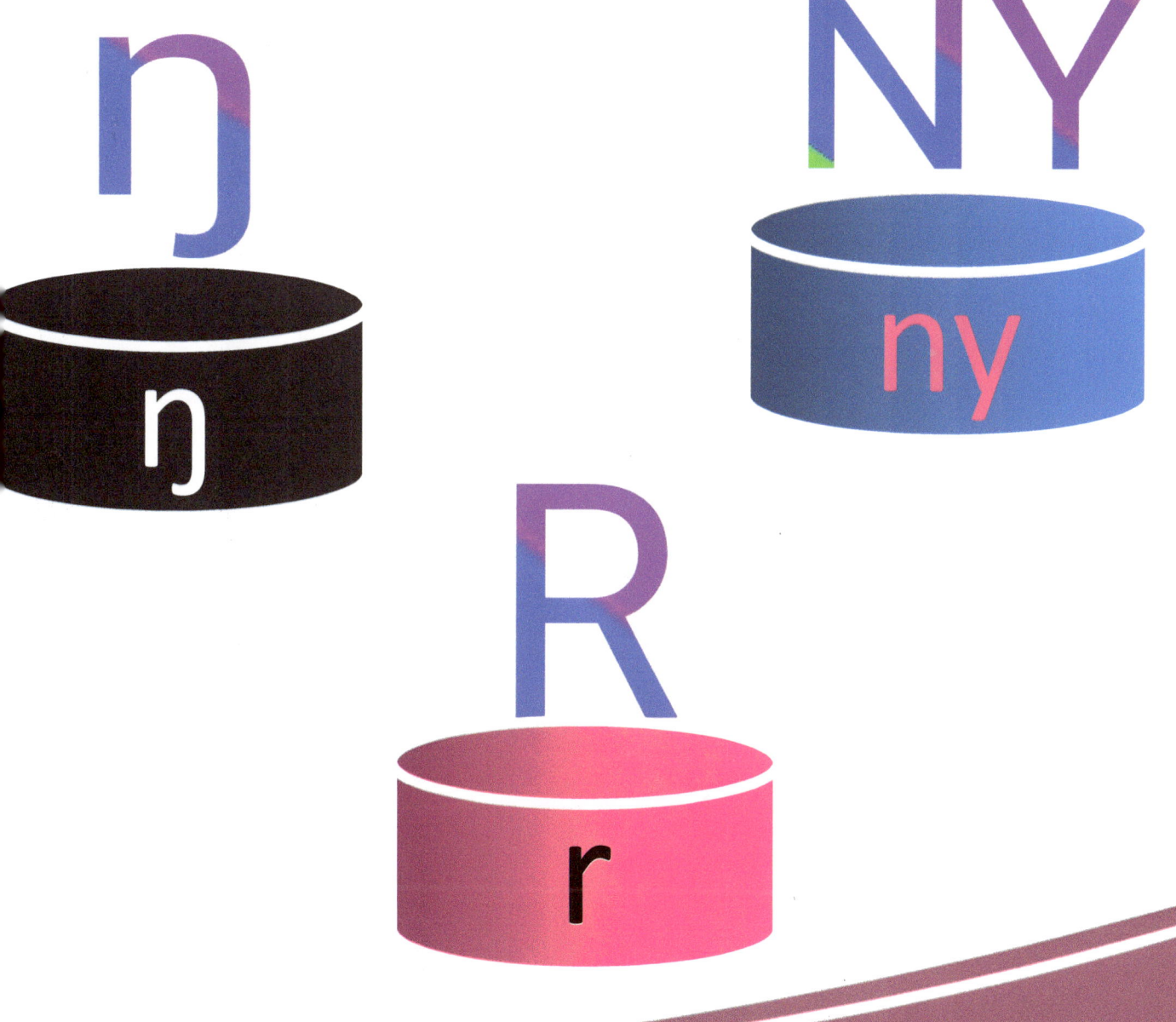

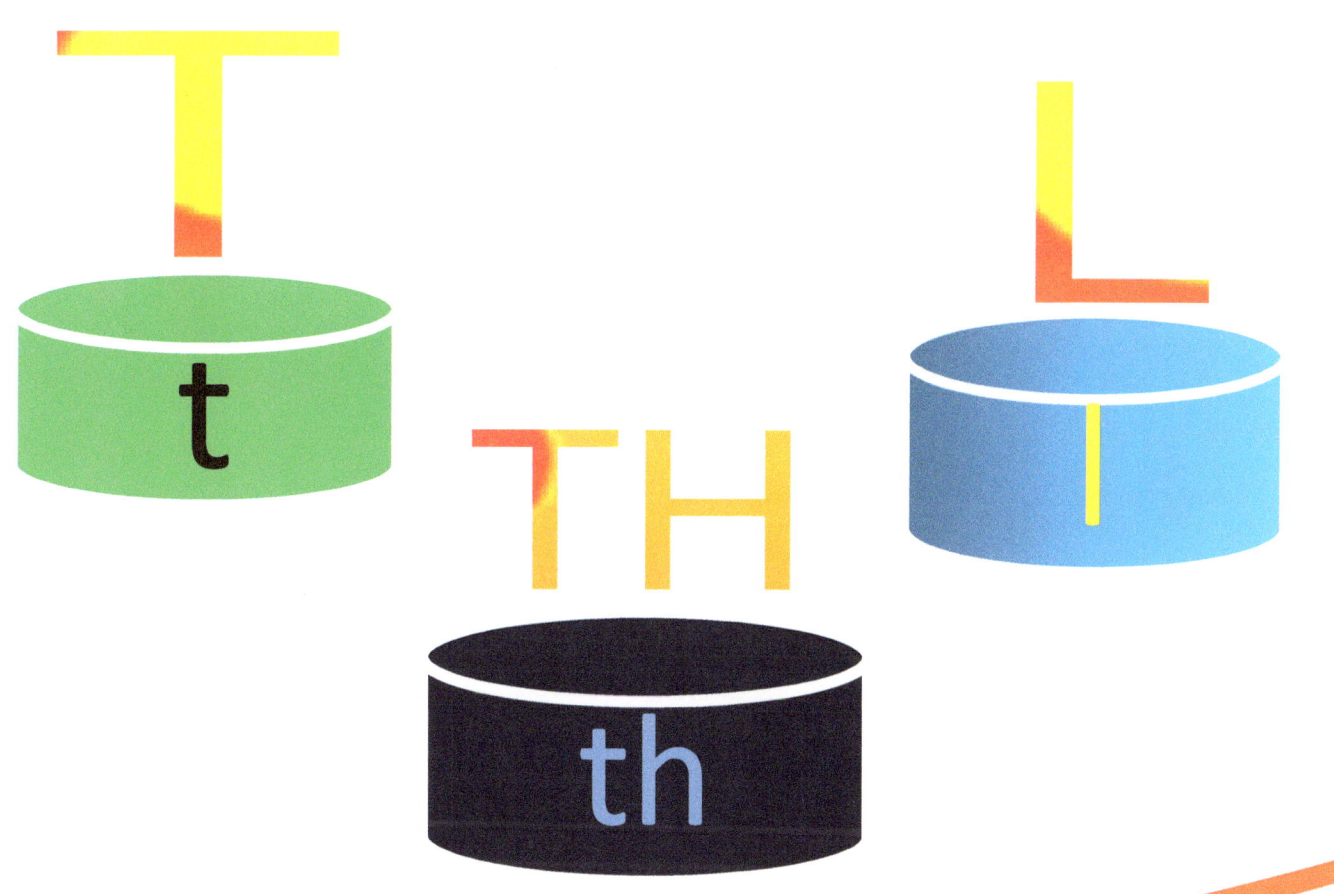

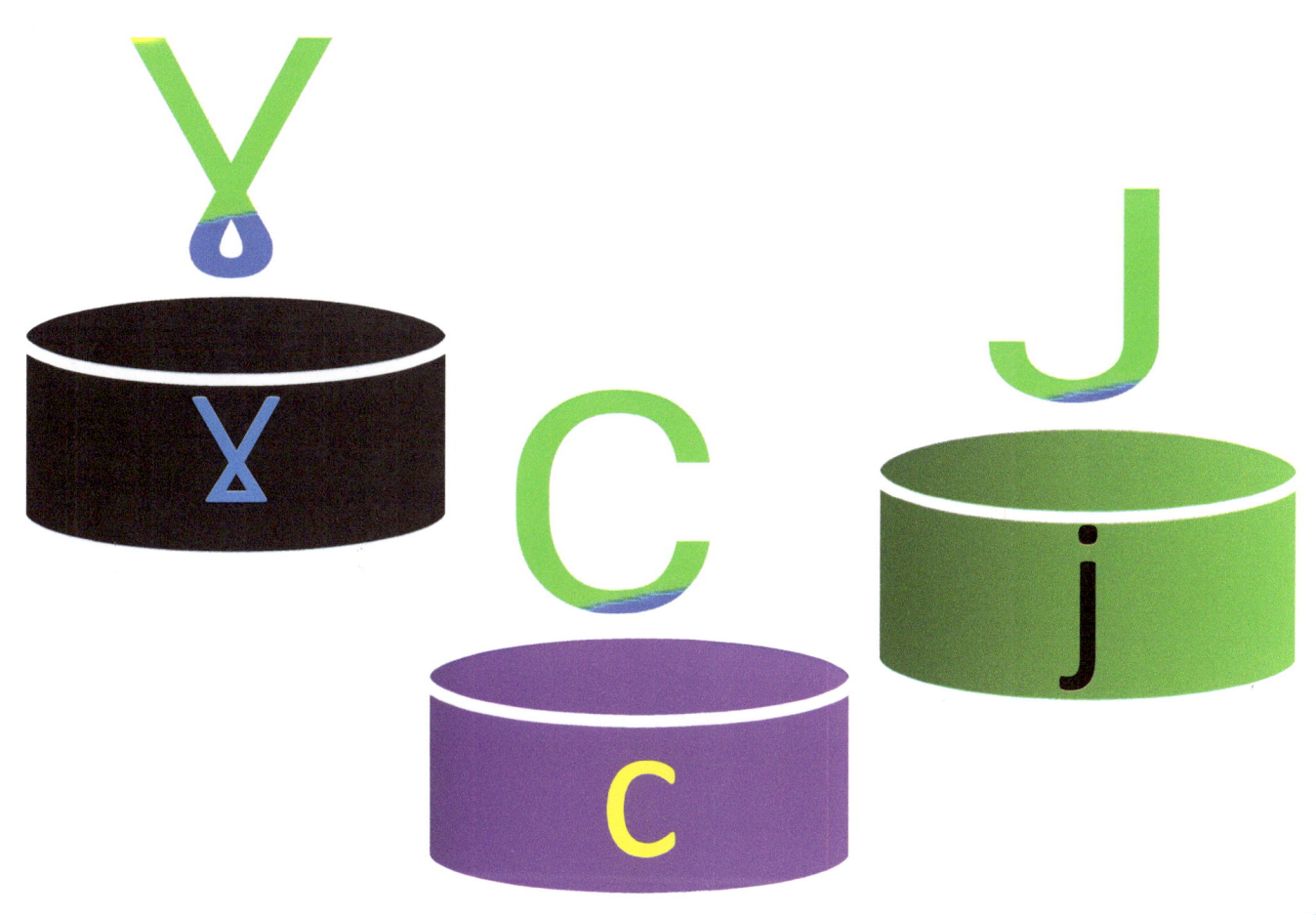

Akeer Dheu

A E I O Ɛ Ɔ

Nyooth de Akeer Dheu

Weŋ

Areu

Theep

Tim

Dom

Miir

Tik

Ariik

Rok

Dom

Thom

Moc

Thoor

Pɛɛi

Ɛ

Alamɛɛt

Kieeth

Areem

Xeer

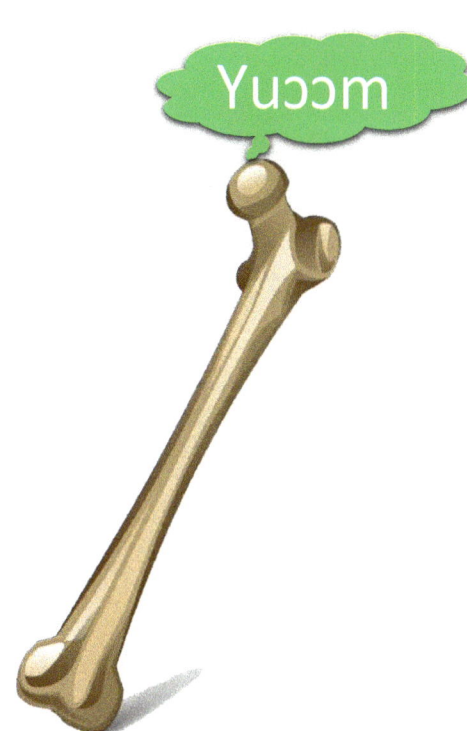
Yuɔɔm

Makuɔɔn

Kɔɔr

Akeer Yäu

Ä Ë Ï Ö Ë Ɔ̈

Nyooth de Akeer Yäu

Aläu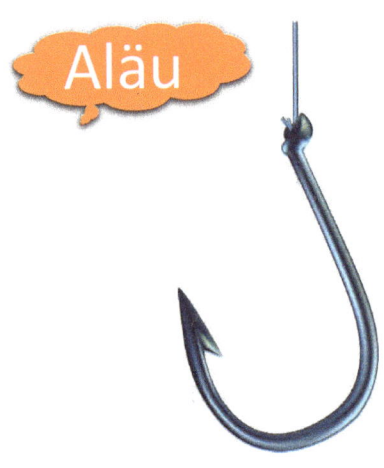

Acëwäth

Cäär

Päny

Määth

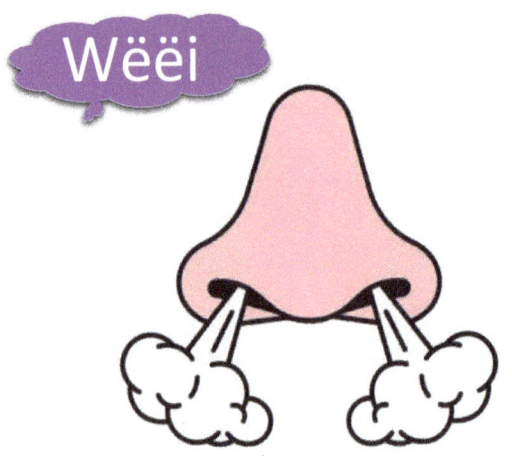

Wëc

Yëu
Yëp

Wëu

 Ajïth

 Rïŋ

Lɔɔ̈r
Bul

Kɔ̈m

Maŋɔ̈ɔ̈r

Akeer Dhëŋ

NH NY DH TH

Nyooth de Akeer Dhëŋ

―――――――

Anyaar

Nyiëël

Nyiny

Nyith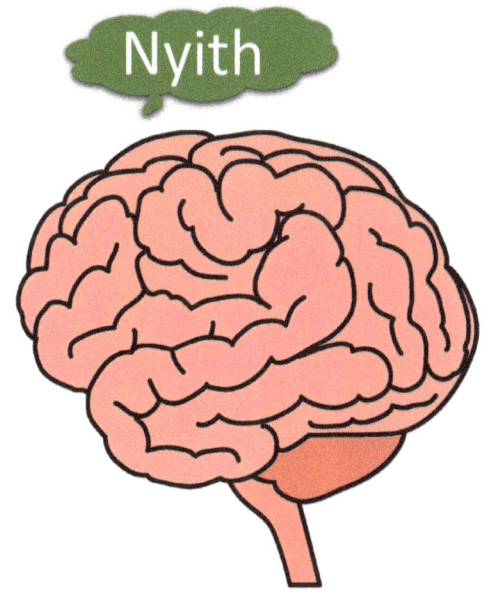

Nyam

Dhuɔŋ

Dhiɔp

Dhiëëu

Thööc

TH

Thuëëc

Thiëu

Thial

Thiëi
Thiëc

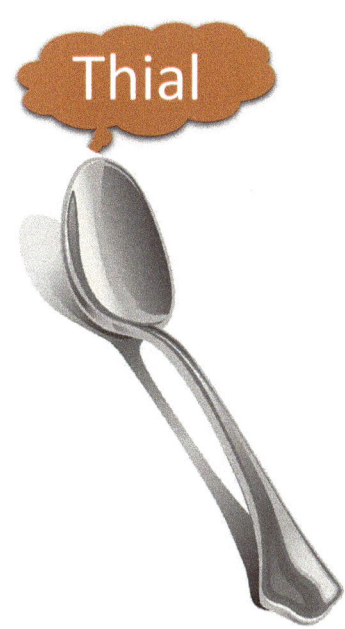

73

Akeer Lɔc

W	Y	B	P	M
N	ŋ	R	D	T
L	K	G	X	C
U				J

Nyooth de Akeer Lɔc

Wum

Wäl

Wëc

Wuɔɔc

Wel

Bap

B

Aboor

Nyancïnbiɔl

Bëër

Bath

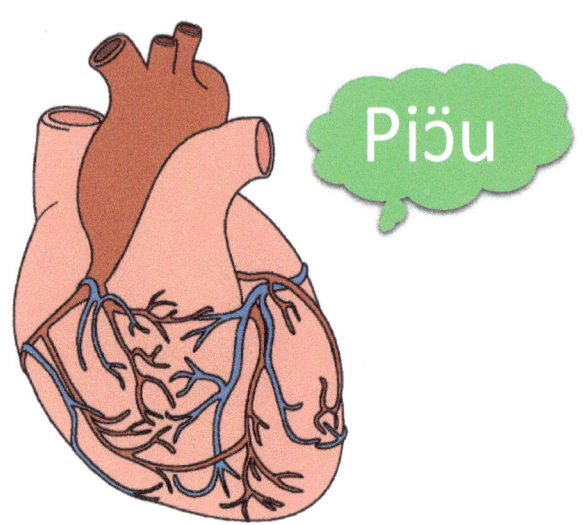

Piɔu

Apet

Amat

M

Miïth

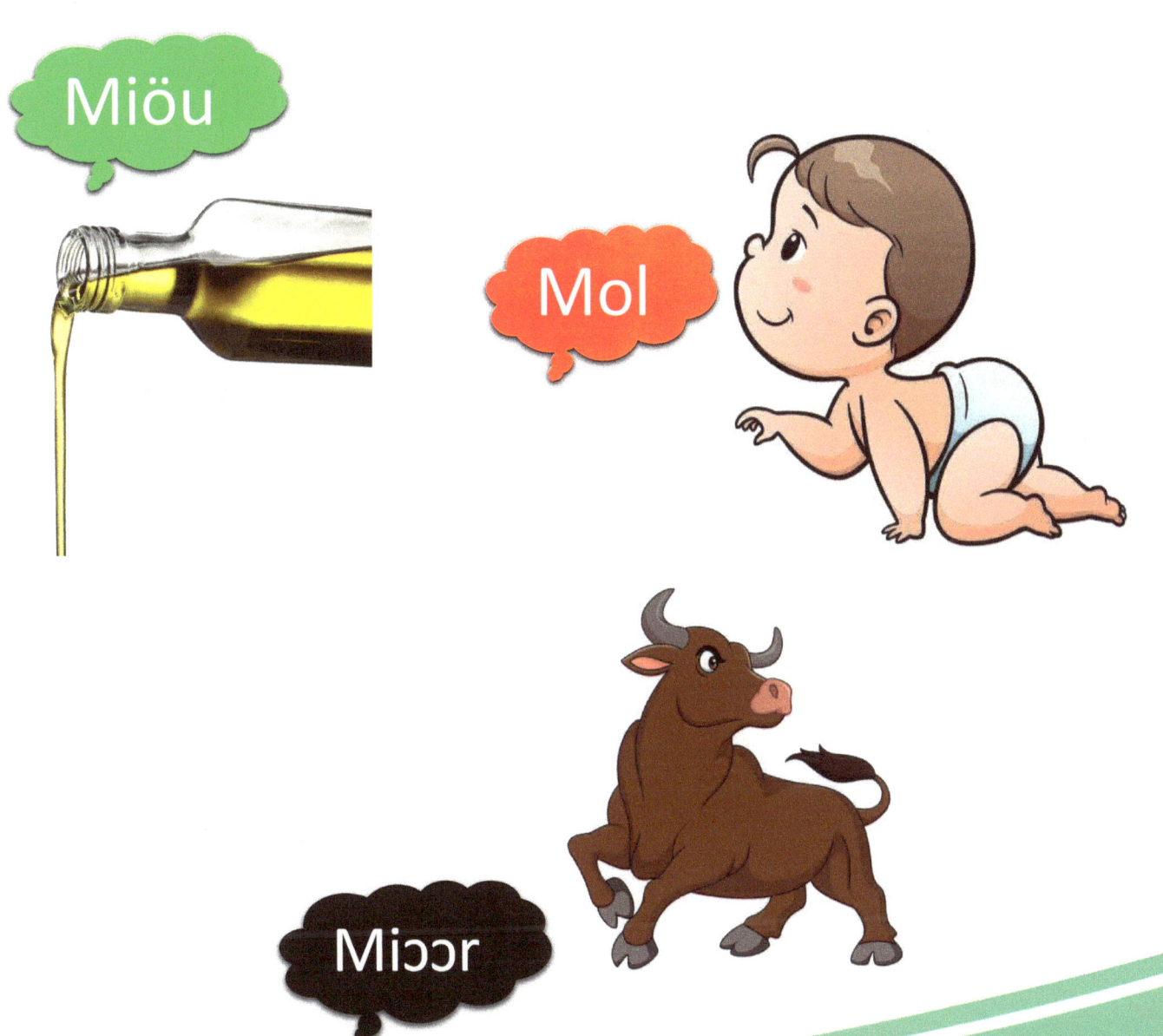

Aŋööt

ŋ

Guŋ

Ruth

Riɛl

Ruɔɔn

Doŋkï

D

Diöny

Löŋ

Lɔ̈ɔm

Këroor

K

Akeu

Kïim

Abaköök

Kët

Guïk

Guεu

Guur

Gut

Goŋ

Xɔɔc

Xɔɔt

Xɛɛc

Cuut

C

Cäm

Cây

Cụm

Cuốc

Kuur

Thuk

Tui

Juääc

Jöt

Jec

Akeer Dheu Ku Akeer Yäu

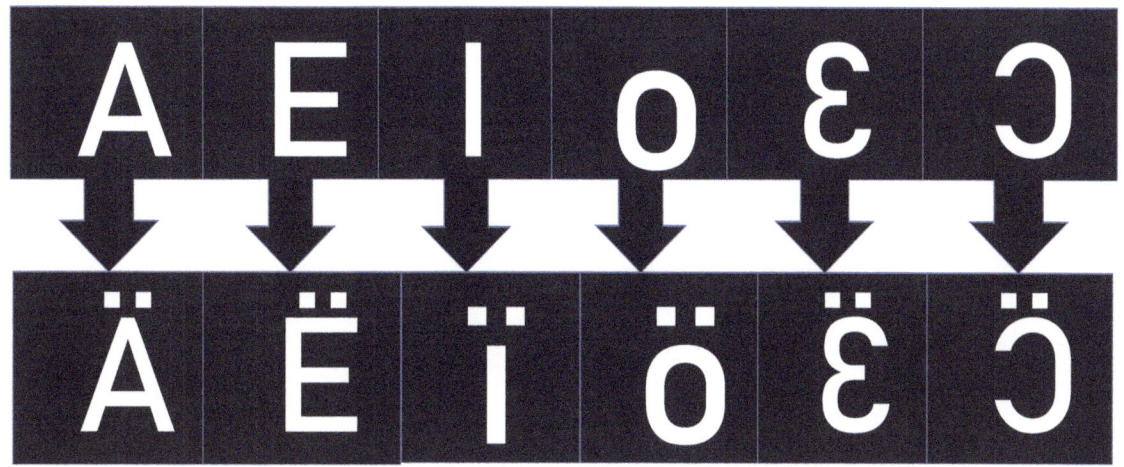

Nyooth de Akeer Dheu ku Akeer Yäu

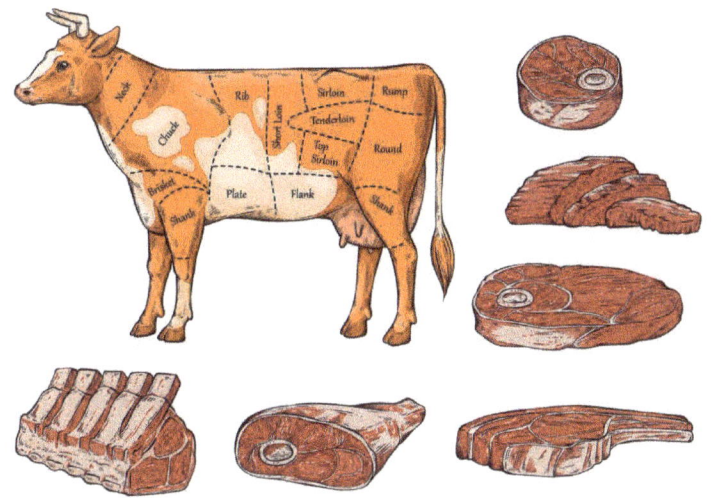

CHAPTER 2

Tök Ku Käjuëc

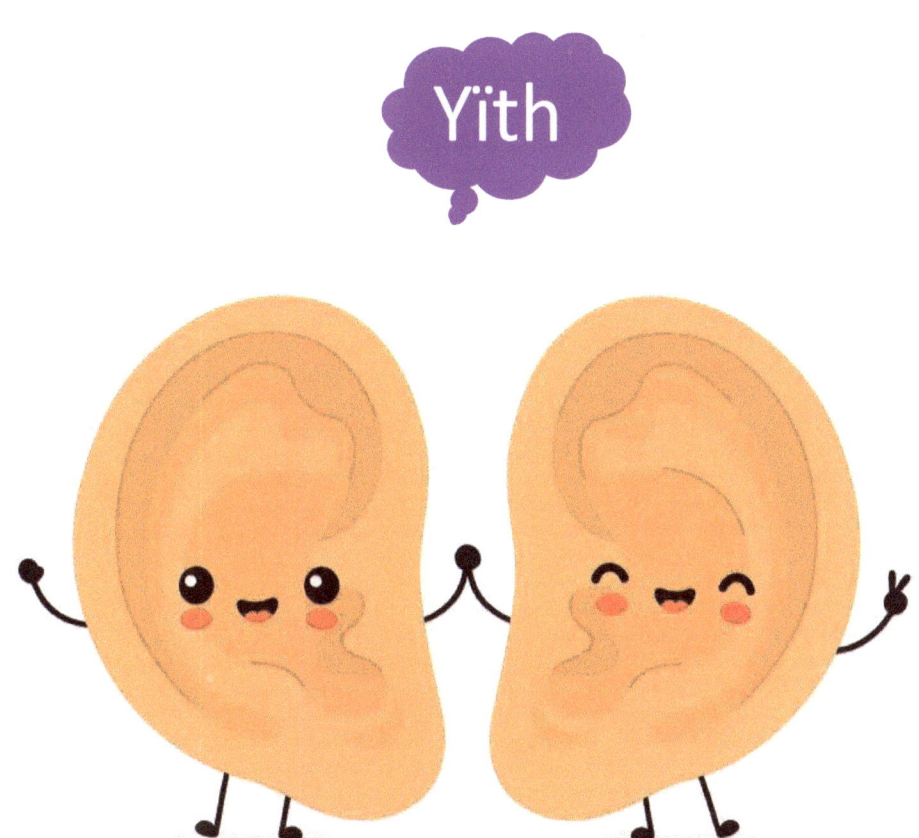

Adhiäät

CHAPTER 3

Ruääi

CHAPTER 4

Kä Tɔ Në Guɔpic

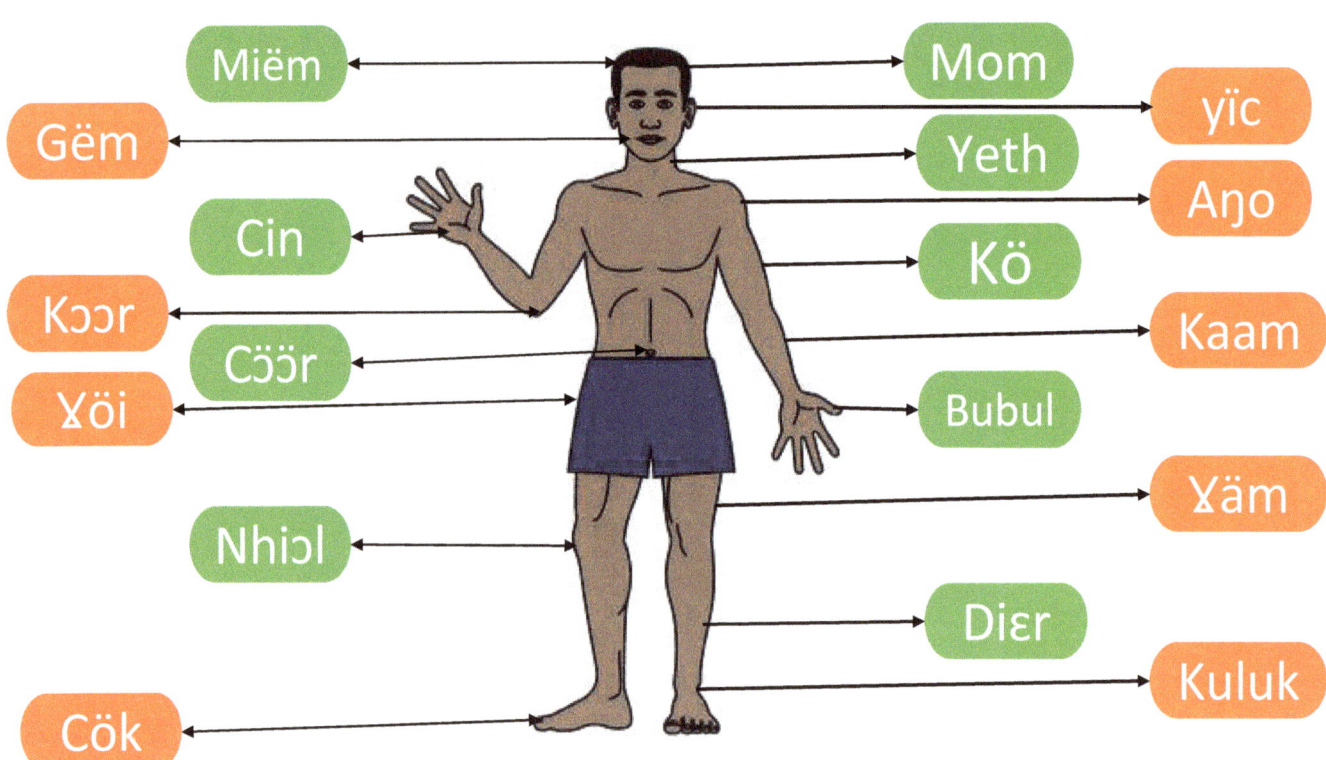

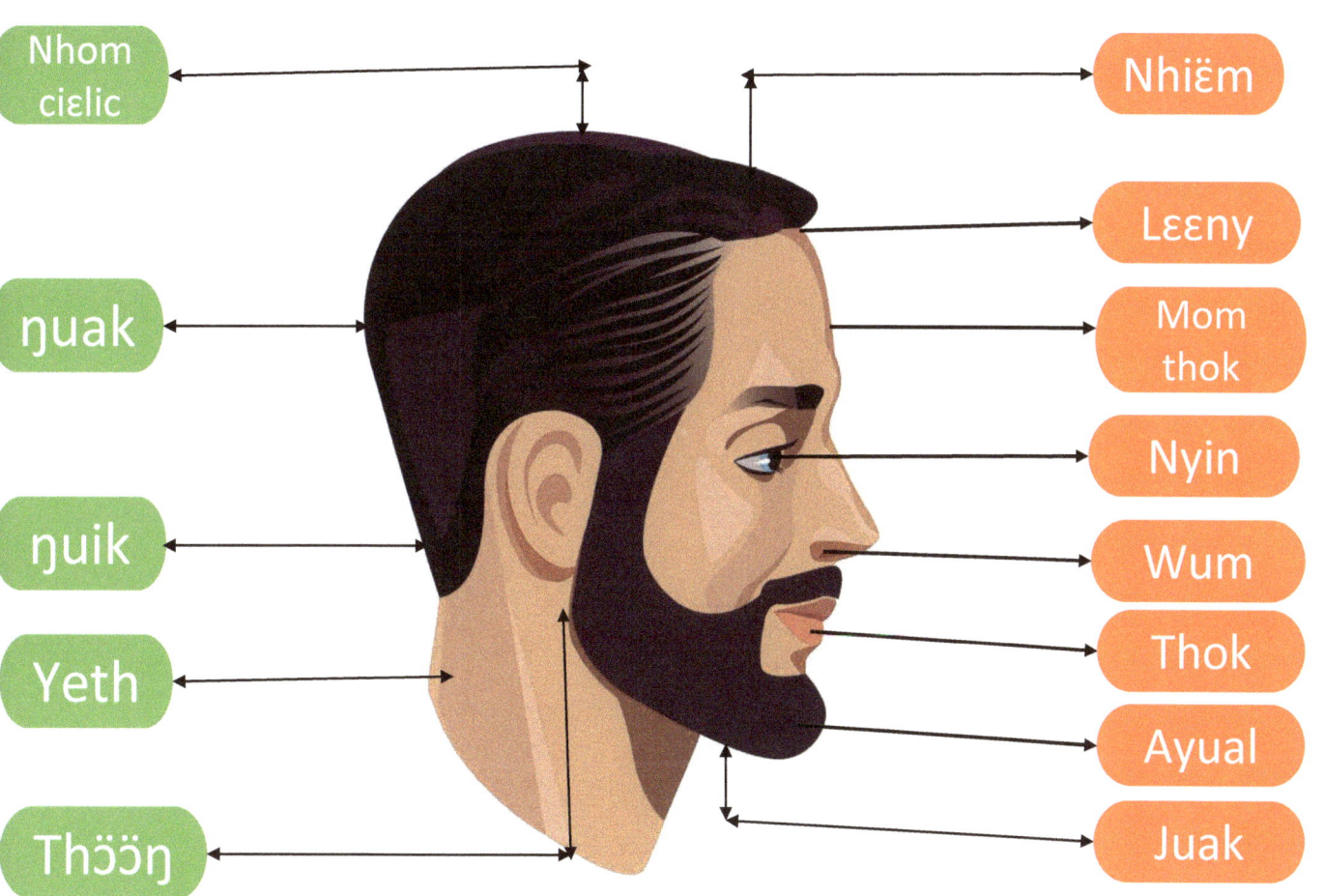

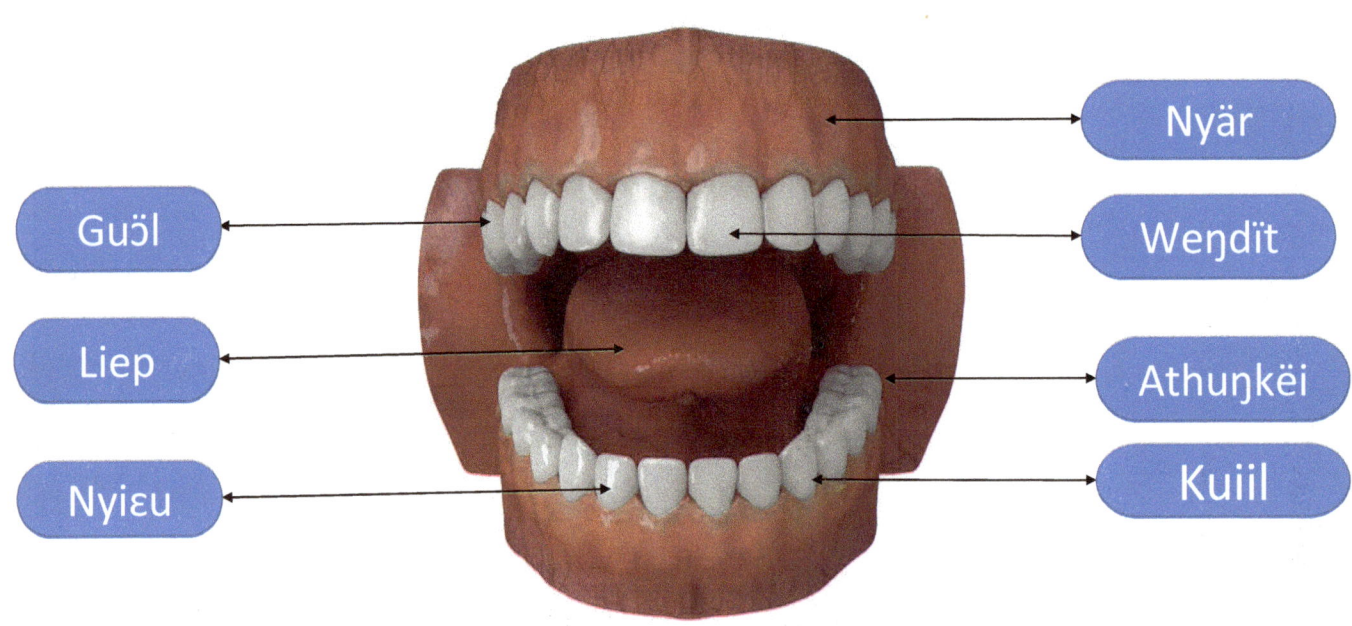

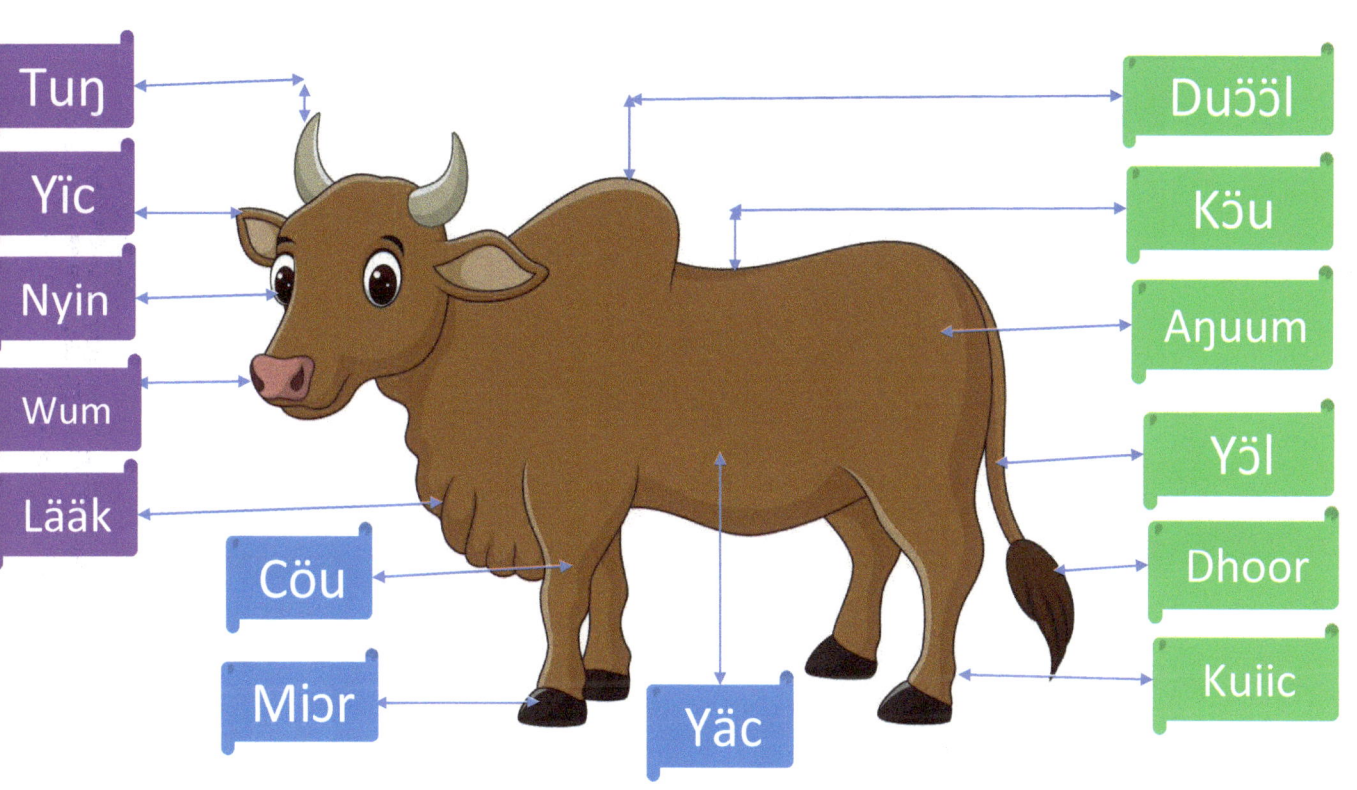

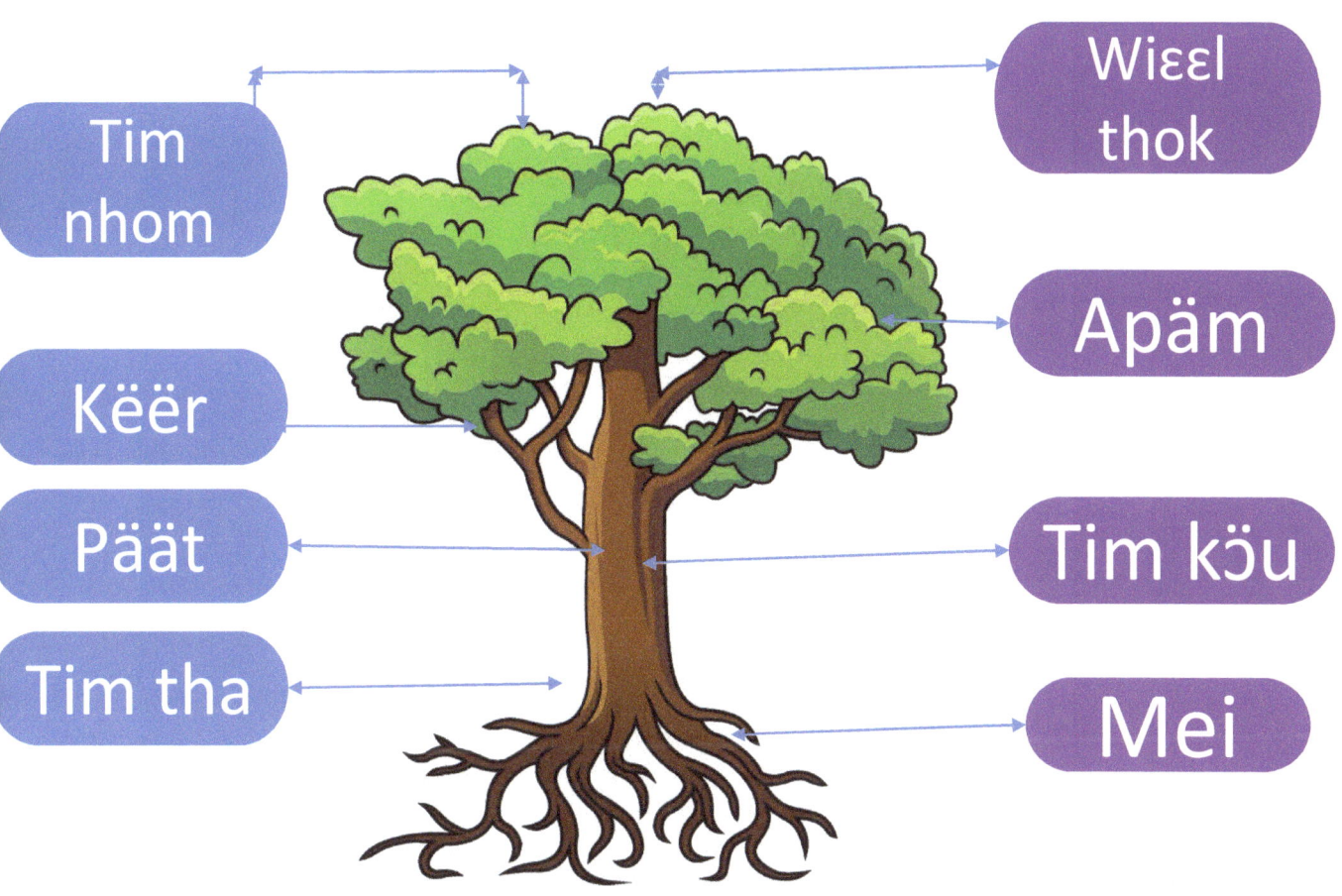

CHAPTER 5

Wël ku Jam

Cämë

Cämkë

Lakë

Pïŋ

Pïŋku

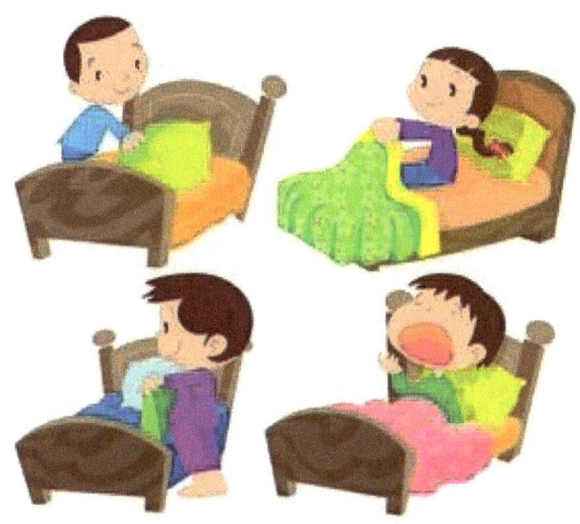

Thiëc

Kudual Mama
Hello mum

Kudual Wënkääi
Hello brother

> Cë yï ruɔ̈n?
> Good morning

> Ca cool?
> **Good afternoon**

Cë yï thëi?
Good evening

CHAPTER 6

Kuɛn

Dhetem

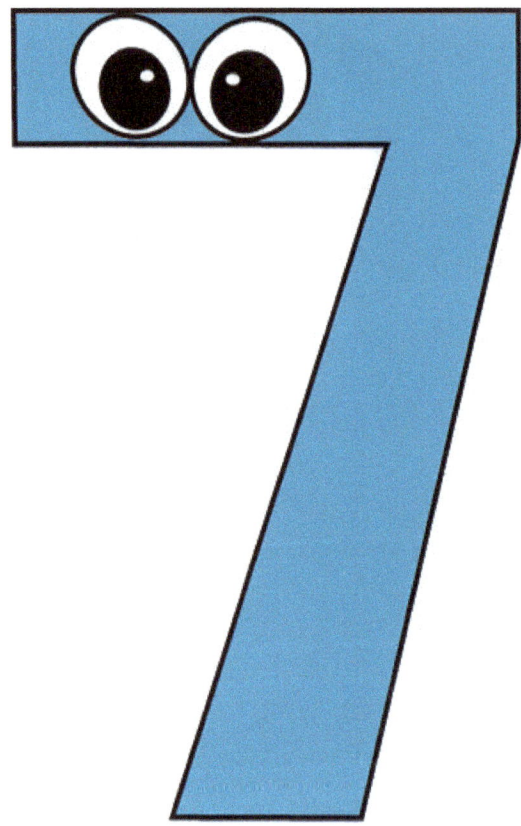

250

Mät

$1 + 1 = 2$

$2 + 1 = 3$

$3 + 1 = 4$

$4 + 1 = 5$

$4 + 2 = 6$

$4 + 3 = 7$

$2 - 2 = 0$

$3 - 2 = 1$

$4 - 2 = 2$

$5 - 2 = 3$

$6 - 2 = 4$

$7 - 2 = 5$

Тёк

$4 \div 1 = 4$

$6 \div 2 = 3$

$8 \div 4 = 2$

$10 \div 2 = 5$

$12 \div 3 = 4$

$14 \div 7 = 2$

Yup

5 x 0 = 0

6 x 1 = 5

7 x 2 = 14

8 x 3 = 24

9 x 4 = 36

10 x 5 = 50

www.ingramcontent.com/pod-product-compliance
Lightning Source LLC
Chambersburg PA
CBHW061804290426
44109CB00031B/2933